Pink Daydreams, Pink Teardrops'

Bhuvi Rajesh

BookLeaf Publishing

India | USA | UK

Made with ❤ on the BookLeaf Publishing Platform
www.bookleafpub.in
www.bookleafpub.com

Dedication

To my mom, I would've never even made it
to the title without you

Acknowledgement

Firstly to my mom for supporting and reminding me over 21 days. To literally every author of every book I've ever read, the artists of every song, and the creators of evry show. My only insparation. To bookleaf publishing for this challenge.

Preface

Writing is difficult but at the same time very easy. This collection is a mix of writings done very easily and some done in the most difficult ways. Some are inspirational, some are filled with humour but some are depressing too. Hope you enjoy reading these as much as I did :)

Poem 1

"You say I dont understand, I say I know you
don't"
-Taylor Swift

You ask me why we don't talk anymore
Or why I never told you this before
Why I kept that secret and so many more
Honey, there's a reason.

I'm living with the fear that it'll be used
against me
If I told you everything, I'd never again be
free
You say I can share everything, but I dissagree
Honey, theres a reason

My aapologies if we have rather dry
conversation
Bit hard to chat when you claim I have an
adiction
And I know I'm closed off, built a reputation
Honey, there's a reason

If you really want to know, I have but one
thing to say
Maybe we'll be open and trusting and honest
one day
But for now, secretive and closed off I shall
stay
Honey, there's a reason

Poem 2

"When it hasn't been your day, your week,
your month or even your year". But I'll be
there for you"
-'Freinds' theme song

It just feels like I'm drowning, in a sea of
sorrow
Death after death, one bad news after another
Sometimes, I hope that, I wont wake up
tommorow
You're the only one who hasnt left me, unlike
the others

Can't remember the last time school has made
me smile
Unlike the rest, who dont dread it as much as
I do
They'll talk and laugh with their freinds,
butit's been a while
That I've talked or laughed with anyone other
than you

I guess life out of school is a bit better, but
truly, not by a lot
Watch as my freinds make inside jokes again,
leaving me out
We make eye contact, guess its always us who
are forgot
You're the only one who I'm truly freinds
with, no doubt

I know, that it's really sad that, you're might
be my only freind
But not for you, I know you're doing bettter,
but not really
We used to be rocky, but you're the only who
I can depend
To always be there,its true, though I know it
sounds silly

Poem 3

Everyone is going to die, no one is going to
remember you. So screw it.
-Billie Eilish
"In front of all those people? I'm not that
daring."
"I could never do that, that's so embarrasing"
Quotes from the insecure, lame and the
boring
Life's too short to overthink and keep on
caring

Who ever regrets taking that risk and going
for it ?
How many regret playing it safe for every
minute?
Toss out hesitation, and those who encourage
it
Life's too short to keep living with all these
limits.

"But what if I fail, and the first try dissapoints
Or I fully flop, going through life
unemployed"

Shake it off, brush it off, dont be so paranoid
Life's too short to always be so worried

Dance your heart out whenever you want to
Sing your lungs out whenever you're feeling
blue
Go with the flow, you'll do what you'll do
Life's too short, so just be you

Poem 4

"Lights, camera and smile. Even when you
want to die"
-Taylor Swift, I Can Do It With A Broken
Heart

Always with the brightest smile in the group
photo
Even when I've been ignored and left out all
day
Smiling and laughing, for reasons I dont even
know
It's the worst time of my life, yet I smile
anyway

I'm not depressed or sad, I'm a complete
physco
For being freindly with people who I wish
would die
I hate everyone here, but I'll smile for the
photo
Not a born liar, a girl adapting to the world
of lies

The world subtly tells you how you should
feel
Crushing anyone who doesnt fit into that
standard
This is the reason why life has no more appeal
Fake smiles, forced laughs, conditioned
answers

Got 4 months of trauma and 4 hours of sleep
About to cry and breakdown, but nobody
knows
Want to break the lie but I'm in too deep
And I want to die, but gotta smile for the
photos

Poem 5

"We want to do a lot of stuff; we're not in great shape. We didn't get a good night's sleep. We're a little depressed. Coffee solves all those problems in one delightful little cup."
-Jerry Seinfeld
Insomnia gifts me bruises under my eyes
Being brutally honest in a world of lies
Smiling while hoping everybody dies
Cause I'm just a sleep deprived girl running on coffee

Losing arguments, thank you sleep deprivation
No energy to waste on a stupid coversation
Starting to hate most human interaction
Cause I'm just a sleep deprived girl running on coffee

Procastinating homework, casue thats my life now
Trying to escape the cycle , but I dont know how

Sleeping when I should study, still passing
somehow
Cause I'm just a sleep deprived girl running
on coffee

Constantly in a state of about to pass out
Constantly filled with anxiety and doubt
Constantly angry enough to yell and shout
Cause I'm just a sleep deprived girl running
on coffee

Poem 6

"We have mirrorballs in the middle of a dance floor, because they reflect light. They are broken a million times, and that's what makes them so shiny. We have people like that in society, too. They hang there, and every time they break, it entertains us"
-Taylor Swift

They watch me as I cry and break down yet again
I try despereatly to collect myself and fail misereably
I hate that I'm just a speactacle for them, even when
My bills get paid for being dramatic and irritable

The gossip articles trash me, but they trash everyone
My own freinds joke about me, but not the real ones
It hurts most that my family sees me as the disapointment

And that my own fans see me as just
entertainment

Does anyone see just me or do they see what
the press says
That I'm a toxic alcholic, who can't hold a job
or a relationship
I know that there are millions who support
me, but I miss the days
Where my freinds wouldnt be sending in
annonymous tips

About my life, all the things I told them in
confidence
Even if I find a trustworty person, I have
none left to give
After all the times it was misplaced, way more
than once
After all the fame, gossip and hate, I just want
to live

Poem 7

What, like it's hard?
-Elle Woods, Legally Blonde

Excuse me for laughing but it is kinda funny
How I ace the hurdle you all find challenging
Make it look so easy, you all look so silly
Trying to make excuses for why I'm winning

Dont get many opprotunities to rub in your
faces
How awesome, intelligent and amazing I
truly am
Excuse my smirk, as you're put in your places
I make winning look so easy, I'm amazing,
dam

Most of the time, I'm barely passing through
Just cause, I'm mostly wasting all my time
But right now, I really want to show you
How amazing I am in truly am sometimes

Actually most times, think that this proves
that

You should be lucky that I barely put effort in
Now, I'm winning straight up, no time for
chit chat
Watch out, I'm coming for you, I like to win

Poem 8

Dam
-Percy Jackson, Titan's Curse
If I'm being honest, the worlds a dam horrible
place
Always dam hard till you find your own space
Lost without it, it's my dam foundation, my
base
Only reason I act with dam dignity and grace

And mine is dam dead trees and ink aka a
book
It's my vibe, my entire dam personality, my
look
Reading it makes anywhere my dam reading
nook
Talking about dam PJO, it's got a special kind
of hook

Reading this, you must think this rhyming
scheme sucks
Like it's so bad, I'd rather get run over by
three dam trucks

The fact something so bad got dam published
is dumb luck
It's dam bad, as bad as stepping into
disgusting, brown muck

Why you gotta be some dam rude to me
I mean, you acting like we dam enemies
Let a girl have some fun, leave me dam be
Dam, just messing around and being free

Poem 9

'As you can see, I am not dead'
-T'challa,Black Panther

Trust me, it's been a rough year or two
No one knows all that hapened but me
I guess they all think that they do
I'm still here but I'll never be free

The deaths that haunt me or the enemies I
picked up along the way
Or all the freinds I lost, and all the freinds I
never had to help me
A world of betrayals, depression, anxiety at
the end of the day
Because, honeslty,with the freinds I've got,
who needs enemies

But it's not like I'm lacking on that front, oh
there is a lot
Of people waiting and watching just to see
me fall
With never enfing insults that seem to lack
any thought

But, as you can see, I'm still standing,alone,
through it all

I've lived with the regret of never being able
to say goodbye
I've lived with too many freinds who do
nothing but lie
I've lived with millions od insults that make
want to die
I've lived, that's my takeaway, which no one
can deny

Poem 10

'I dont regret,just pretend shit never
happened'
-Good Days, SZA

'I dont regret, just pretend shit never
happened'
I'm regretting pretending that shit never
happened
Should've never gone along with your game of
pretend
Misscommunication is how most freindships
end

I'm new in this group, but seems like this is
the norm
That after every big fight, pretend nothing
went wrong
Brushing past like it's nothing, I would hate
to inform
Is how this group will fall apart, it wont be to
long

Before fights break out, simply because of
built up issues
"How do you know?'" cause it's happened too
many times
Fights that end in screaming and a whole box
of tissues
I guess, just letting it go isin't the solution
sometimes

Poem 11

That's just the way life goes. I like to slam
doors closed. Trust me, I know it's always
about me
-Gracie Abrams, I Love You I'm Sorry

I know, that I caused all of the issues cause
I'm always dramatic
I know, it's my fault for digging up the past,
not letting things die
I know, I shouldn't have re-opened old
wounds, to be poetic
I know, it was perfect before me and I ruined
it all, no need to lie

Do you think, I wouldnt know all the things
you said behind my back
Do you think, that your secret meetings and
polls would just stay hidden
Don't you think, that trying to kick me out of
the group is a personal attack
Don't you think, that if you said this to my
face, than I would listen

But I wouldnt blame you, I know I'm an issue,
a walking bomb
One word bad about me and I'll explode in an
instant,all over town
And I'll scream and I'll scream, from 6-feet
under in the tomb
Because the second you betrayed and
back-stabbed me, I went down

The worst thing is, I know I'm always to
blame, and rightfully so
Wasn't I the one who pushed them away, and
so many more
When it comes to destroying relationships,
could say I'm a pro
And I act like I couldn't care less, but I've
never been hurt more

Poem 12

Har ghadi badal rahi hai roop zindagi.Chaon
hai kabhi, kabhi hai dhoop zindagi.Har pal
yahan jee bhar jiyo.Joh hai samaan kal ho naa
ho.
-SRK,Kal Ho Naa Ho
I see you there, quietly hiding under the shade
Staying in you comfort zone simply cause
you're afraid
Dont you know what's lost cause of chances
delayed
Dont you know you're going to regret having
stayed

Im not going to lie, tell you everythings easy
And all you have to do is just believe in
yourself
No, I'm not gonna say it's gonna be light and
breezy
But opportunities won't just present themsel

You could stay depressed, but stil in your safe
zone

Not remembering the last time a smile was on
your face
Or go out, party, have fun, with freinds or
even alone
Life is a beautiful chaos you just have to
embrace

So quit being upset or always angry with the
world
Toss the negative attitude, and stop saying 'no'
And just look at the new opportunities that
unfurled
Just smile, laugh and life life, kal ho naa ho

Poem 13

"Indifference and neglect often do much
more damage than outright dislike."
-Albus Dumbledore, Harry Potter

Are we friends, or do you secretly despise me
Are you one of the ones who find me
annoying
Doubts and signs, red flags in front of me
But theyre just assumptions, cause I'm just
guessing

That one girl, who no matter the situation
Every time we speak at any social occasion
Each and every sentence, snarky and sarcastic
Its like she's always rude and condescending
Everyone says that she's so cool and epic
I'd say she hates me, but I'm just guessing

But she can be excused, we're simply
acquaintances
Though for another, we meet on a daily basis
Comments and jokes, all completely
unnecessary

Anger issues and temper, she thinks she's
funny
No one fights her, she thinks its cause she's
scary
It's cause she's so stubborn, no one has the
energy

Cause it's going towards school, another
problem
Annoying idiots, and "friends" who side with
them
It's not like I'm asking you to fight for me
But don't go and side with the my enemy
I'll sound immature, till you hear her laughing
I don't think we're friends anymore, at least
I'm guessing

They secretly hate me, that's my conclusion
But with no hard text, it's just an assumption
With no direct words, one reads between the
lines
And what I'm reading is that they've crossed
the line
It could be a miscommunication, I'm just
guessing

But I don't want to stay if I have to keep
guessing

Poem 14

I might not feel real, but it's okay
-Gracie Abrams, I Love You I'm Sorry
Got a few personalities, which one am I
faking
Just Smile as I pretend my hearts not
breaking
Contemplate life with each breath that I'm
taking
Too many feelings that leave me crying and
shaking

I Guess it'll feels like I'm drowning, alone in a
sea
That will always keep growing, I'll never be
free
Each breath could be my last, the sea drowns
out my plea
This world leaves me fuming, screaing like a
banshee

But I dance through the song, and I'll dance
through the night

And I'll joke, and I'll laugh, I'll sing like
everythings alright
Happy,positive and bubbly, even as I'm losing
the fight
The fight for my sanity, which I'm losing as I
write

Play therapist for my freinds, though I'm the
one who needs it
Feel like I'm dying, slowly losing my mind,
that I will admit
Sleep is my escape, my heaven, only as much
as time'll permit
After that, it seems like I'm a charachter,
playing a part in a skit

Poem 15

We are the world. We are the children. We are
the ones who make a brighter day.
-Micheal Jackson, We Are The World

The sparkling ocean's gorgeous sound
Has me wondering and looking all around
With miles of sands stretching long
This beautiful fantasy just feels wrong

Inland we go,through a forest of trees
Rays of light break through the towering
leaves
Vines creep up and critters scramble around
So is the beautiful ways of the nature that
surrounds

In extreme north and south in the land of
snow and bitter cold
With icy peaks and lovely skies , it as many
wonders to be told
In masses and acres of snowy white the night
sky has a colourful surprise

Up across massive hills , a starry fantasy, in
these poles , the lights arise

Throughout the world nature shows her
surprise
From long sunny beaches to to areas of
freezing ice
In a jungle of trees and a wide land of grass
It's now up to us to make this world last

Poem 16

Lies are comforting. Truth is painful.
-Xaden Riorson, Fourth Wing
Lies are comforting, truth is painful, and
that's a fact
Why do you think most people hate me so
much
I don't sugarcoat or lie, so they feel attacked
Because I'm not blindly complimenting, as
such

In a world made of lies, one has but two
choices
Adapt and be liked, or be honest and despised
I choose the second,choose not to hide my
voice
For the angels are devils, hiding in a disguise

You can say I'm a brutal monster, that I have
no heart
And I may agree with you, but one thing is
true is that
There is no one worse than a person with a
stone heart

Who's words are sweeter than sugar, they're
worse than a rat

I know that I am definitely not the nicest or
sweetest
But one thing I'll say is that I am absulutely
honest
For the 'angels' will lie to your face and you'll
say they're the best
But me, I say the truth, and I'm the one you
all will detest

Poem 17

I will not die today.
-Violet Sorrengail, Fourth Wing

If you think I made it so far to be taken down
by you
You definitely picked the wrong girl, thats
true
If you knew half of the shit I've been through
Maybe you'll know, I will not die today

Death after death, betrayals, always drowning
in regrets
But I'm stubborn as a stone, sorry if that
makes you upset
I never lose a fight, and don't give in to empty
threats
Sorry, but I will not die today

I may have lost once, twice or maybe even
thrice
But I'm still standing, it shouldnt really be a
suprise

You're nothing but an annoyance, would you
like a prize?
For losing of course, I will not die today

I can't help but smirk at the look on your face
As I look behind at you, winning the race
I win with humility and with a whole lot of
grace
Like I said, I will not die today

Poem 18

The only thing worse than being blind is
having sight but no vision
-Helen Keller

Imagine a world where all is dark
There's nothing to do but listen to others
snark
To hear their cruel words cut through silence
For you have this strange thing called
blindness

They say they are 'open' and 'free-thinking'
They say it doesn't matter, but who are they
kidding
Because they pity me; are scared of
judging me
No one really wants to be friends with me

Honestly, I am the one who's truly
free-spirited
When you can't see, your thoughts aren't
limited

No matter your skin colour, gender or
anything
It truly doesnt matter, cause I can see see
nothing

It's obviously hard and pretty frustrating
"Why me" is what I am left thinking
But really I am fine, not a huge mess
I'm a lot like you, or them or anyone else

Poem 19

If I cannot be better than them, I will become
so much worse.
-Jude Duarte, Cruel Prince

Do you think, I always the rude, mean and
sarcastic
I remember once, when I was happy and
enthusiastic
Must've been something, to turn the optimist
into skeptic
Now I'm mistrusful of everyone, must be
fantastic

Sometimes I miss the girl I was, so sweet and
kind
At least till I remember what made her into
the girl today
Small, stupid insults that made their way into
my mind
The kind of experiences that dont, and wont,
just go away

I remember the first time I realised he
changed me
That a simple word could trigger such intense
hostility
No, it wasn't just a stupid boy, a bully or an
enemy
He , or they, forced me to abandon all of my
fragility

Any weakness can be used for one more insult
Civilty doesn't diffuse, it escalates the
situation
Hate that is still lasts, but can't argue with the
result
This is what changed me into this, for your
information

Poem 20

Life is unpredictible. Not everything's in our
control. But as long as we're with the right
people, we can handle anything
-Amy Santiago, Brooklyn Nine Nine

I still remember, when everything in my life
changed
New school, new house, new life, but months
of hurt
I remember a constant, the only one who
remained
As the rest left, leaving me stranded in a
dessert

She was there, when ever I wanted to trauma
vent
Or even when I wanted to spill tea about
random things
We had a rocky past, but right now, in the
present
I can talk to her about everything and
anything

I think she feels the same, as I talk as much as
listen
From harmless discussions about our mutual
interests
To having depressing, deep and honest
discussions
With stupid, light hearted joint boards on
Pintereast

Thank you, for letting me vent about
litereally everything
Thank you, for never giving me any kind of
doubt
That we werent freinds, I'm always happy
after meeting
you to chat, you're the only one who's never
left me out

2I

Today's A Dog's Birthday. A Very Special Day
-Bhuvi Rajesh

Today's a dogs birthday
A very special day
Today's a day dog was born
Today's a dogs birthday

Today's a day to celebrate

A day full of joy
And cake and songs
For a dog, girl and boy

Happy Birthday , dear dog
You should very proud
This day is just perfect
The song is perfectly loud

Today's a dog's birthday
A very special day
Today's a day a dog was born
Today's a dog's birthday